The Commentators
24 Hour Scalextric
Tuning Out With Radio Z

**durational performances and a play
by Stan's Cafe**

ISBN 978-1-913185-22-0

Published by Stan's Cafe
Birmingham, UK
2020

www.stanscafe.co.uk

24 Hour Scalextric © Stan's Cafe 2009
Photos pg 3 © Jonathan Stokes
Pgs 4, 5, 6, 7 © Stan's Cafe
The Commentators © Stan's Cafe 2009
Photos pgs 10, 19, 24, 28, 37 © Graeme Braidwood
Pgs 12, 13, 26, 31, 32, 40 © Stan's Cafe
Pg 15 © Simon Hanson
Pg 18 © Ming De Nasty
Pg 29 © Lee Allen
Tuning Out With Radio Z © Stan's Cafe 2010
Photos pgs 48, 53, 55, 66, 80 © James Yarker
Pgs 53, 57, 58, 60, 64, 68, 74 © Graeme Braidwood
Publication © Stan's Cafe 2020

Contents:

24 Hour Scalextric
The Event   2
The Consequences   6
Extract of blog post Digital Play   8
24 Hour Scalextric: Media Release   9

The Commentators   10

Tuning Out With Radio Z   48
Early thinking   51
Sleeper instructions   57
Technical specifications   61
Performing *Tuning Out With Radio Z*   64
Original flier and programme   70
Warwick Arts Centre playlists   73
Reviews   75
Blob post   76
Notes on video for Liam   77
Themes and actors   81

24 Hour Scalextric

The Event

At last we had our own venue and all the freedom that this brought. We could do anything we wanted, all the things that conventional venues could never let us do, such as... Well that was the big question, such as what?

We had been searching for our own dedicated rehearsal space ever since our bleak unit on New Canal Street had been bulldozed to make way for a library that was never built. Now the metal workers A. E. Harris & Co. had agreed to rent us a set of four interconnected workshop spaces on the south east corner of their site, allowing us to mount a big version of our installation, *Of All The People In All The World*. We loved the space so much that when the installation was over we didn't move out. The space was much bigger than anything we had ever imagined taking on but it was just about affordable and it opened possibilities for us to do so much... If only we could decide what.

I'd never had Scalextric at home, so I'd always always had to go round to other people's houses to play. The best track was at a friend's where they sent it out onto the landing, disrupting household life, before diverting it back into their bedroom.

Now we had our own money and our own factory home there was nothing to stop us building an enormous Scalextric track and staying up all night racing. It was a whimsical, self-indulgent idea but it wouldn't go away.

Clearly an epic length race track would deserve an epic length race. *24 hours of Le Mans* is the iconic long race and the perfect model for our model race. It was decided. We would buy second hand kit, build a great track, erect our seating bank and have two teams race each other for 24 hours, coinciding with the full size French version in June.

The one remaining sticking point was a justification. Why would we do this? What would make it art? We weren't satisfied in the Duchampian argument that by calling it art we could make it art, we wanted an extra layer.

This was 2009 and internet radio was just ceasing to be an entirely niche enterprise, we recognised that by supplying audiences with an online commentary of the race we could extend our audience, explore this new media and give the whole event an artistic rationale.

We built and tested our track, tinkered with it and tested it some more. It was spectacularly temperamental. We arranged catering and films and activities for kids and families. We got the internet radio hook-up sorted out. We bought two old sheepskin coats and rented two lip-mics. We built the seating bank and invited an audience.

People came. There was an initial rush at the opening that sustained through the afternoon and into the evening. Enthusiasts stayed into the night. It was drivers and marshals only in the small hours but at dawn more people started gathering for breakfast and brunch until, approaching two in the afternoon, a decent crowd was around to be showered with champagne as Jack Trow was hailed the winning driver.

The Consequences

Broadly speaking there are two categories of scientific research. Scientists either set off to discover something they know will have useful applications should they succeed in find it, or they set off to explore an interesting field where they have no preconceived notions of how any discoveries may be applied. *24 Hour Scalextric* was an experimental performance of the second category.

The artistic discoveries made through staging this whimsical, self-indulgent performance had three entirely unexpected outcomes:

1: A teacher visiting the performance spotted all the educational potential of staging smaller versions of the event in schools. The track and the races are full of maths: angles and measurements, timings and calculations. The invitations, commentary and sports reports are full of literacy challenges. Students are required to practice team work and practical skills. All of this legitimate learning is a spin-off activity that had utterly engrossed his kids.

As a consequence we started staging Scalextric races in schools as part of our Creative Learning programme.

2: How audiences responded to the gulf between the live and mediated event was fascinating. People who heard the commentary before they saw the race were underwhelmed by the ramshackle reality in comparison to their mental image. In contrast those people who saw the race first enjoyed the gulf between their experience and what was described to them in the commentary.

This tension between live presence and mediated presence directly inspired our next studio theatre production *Tuning Out With Radio Z* (2010).

3: Audiences seemed to love the commentators both at home (where data suggests they listened for hours at a time) and in the venue. We'd assumed people would find the commentary irritating but the opposite was the case people found it compelling.

Almost immediately the commentators got their first external booking and became The Commentators.

Extract of blog post *Digital Play*

"Then there are those projects who are seeing digital as a medium in its own right – the wonderfully simple but brilliantly engaging *Everyday Moments* by Fuel or (a personal favourite – unsurprising given my love of cricket commentary) Stan's Cafe 'commentaries' – both of sports games and of artistic events (art gallery openings, ballet first nights).

The commentaries are interestingly a good example of something that #digicaparts speaker @nicoleyershon touched on – the importance of playing and experimenting. The commentary programme emerged from a seemingly ridiculous experiment (a 24 Hour Scalextric [race]) in 2009 which became almost legendary."

Matthew Linley
27 March, 2012
Matthewlinley.wordpress.com

24 Hour Scalextric: Media Release

Stan's Cafe presents
24 Hour Scalextric
@ A.E. Harris, 110 Northwood Street, Birmingham
13 June: 13:00 doors open – 14.00 race starts
– 22.00 closed to public
14 June: 10:00 venue open to public
–14:00 chequered flag & awards.

Timed to coincide with the official Le-Mans 24 Hour race, theatre company Stan's Cafe have converted their factory Headquarters in Birmingham's Jewellery Quarter into the site of a major Scalextric track and invited six teams to battle it out though a gruelling 24 hours of slot-car racing.

This extraordinary race will be surrounded by a host of activities:
Family arts workshops.
Films screened by 7" Cinema and Outer Sight.
Pitstop Cafe run by Kitchen Garden Cafe.
Surprise guests.
Scalextric test tracks for public participation.

Visitors can watch the race unfold from the Grandstand and followed around the globe as a full, uninterrupted live commentary is provided by Stan's Cafe directors Craig Stephens and James Yarker, and streamed online from.

On the Sunday morning visitors will be able to come and join the teams for brunch as we count down to see who will win the coveted 24 Hour Scalextric Trophy.

Everyone is invited, live or over the web, to be part of one of the most memorable events of the sporting / artistic year.

Entrance charge - £2 Adults/£1 Children
Weekend tickets -£5/£2.50

The Commentators

On 13th June, 2009 at 2pm Craig Stephens and I started what was to be an unbroken commentary on a 24 hour long Scalextric race. We started this commentary as ourselves but by its conclusion it was clear that we had inadvertently developed twin alter egos – The Commentators.

We were surprised by how popular The Commentator were. We had imagined they would just be irritating but people had listened to them for hours at home streamed over the internet and asked for speakers to be turned up in the venue so that their commentary could be heard more clearly.

Now that Gavin Wade at Eastside Projects had enquired about booking The Commentators to perform at one of the gallery's openings they had clearly become an act in their own right, separate from the Scalextric race.

We took the financial gamble of buying two beautiful but expensive Coles commentator lip-mics, assuming that more work would follow on from the gallery opening.

We gave The Commentators a fictional backstory, that they were once famous sports commentators who have fallen on hard times and are now forced to take any commentary job that came their way, no matter how unlikely.

Intriguingly, in the COVID19 lockdown of 2020 this fictional scenario played out in real life with genuine sports commentators reduced to sharing commentaries of domestic activities on social media.

The Commentators Call: Eastside Gallery Opening
Graeme Rose and Craig Stephens
Commissioned by Eastside Projects (2009)

From a position above the action The Commentators kept listeners up to date with all the comings and goings at the opening of the *Abstract Cabinet* show, who was drinking how much wine or beer and who was talking to whom.

The Commentators Call: Brazil v Portugal
Craig Stephens and James Yarker
Technical help: Howard Potts
Commissioned by Fierce (2010)

Freshly into their tenure as co-Directors of Fierce Laura McDermot and Harun Morrison invited The Commentators to be part of their first festival. They were keen to promote teaser performances that would have a fuller manifestation within the festival.

Harun suggested that we commentate on coverage of the 2010 World Cup. In keeping with the 'rule' that The Commentators no longer get invited to commentate on top level sport, it was agreed that they should not be able to see the match, instead they would attempt to intuit match action from the responses of a crowd watching the event on a big screen.

So The Commentators sat at a table in the Warwick University Students' Union with a clear view of a crowd of students engrossed in the Portugal vs Brazil Group G game. Their commentary was then fed through to the Mead Gallery at Warwick Arts Centre, where it was played over television coverage of the match, hopelessly out of synch and inaccurate.

The Commentators Call: Broad Street
Craig Stephens and James Yarker
With help from Peter Maxwell Dixon
Commissioned by Fierce (2011)

A varied set of six commentaries were agreed with Fierce for their 2011 festival, but logistical issues meant only one came to fruition. This was an overnight (18:00 - 06:00) commentary of action on Broad Street, Birmingham's most popular nightclub destination, renowned for the reeling drunkenness of its patrons come the early hours.

Finding a good vantage point for our Broad Street commentary proved difficult, so we reverted to a fall back option of booking a hotel room overlooking the street. This option was itself undermined by the fact that all the local hotels are all designed to protect their guests from the riotous noise of Broad Street and so we couldn't find a single room over looking the action. Instead, we had to settle for a much better option, a room overlooking a gravel strewn NCP car park with, to our far left a sight of a small section of Broad Street, comprising some building site hoardings and four fast food establishments.

Craig was on fire, powering through the nocturnal twelve hours. James was in all sorts of trouble, speaking through a fug of fatigue and intermittently overwhelmed by sleep.

We couldn't help but wonder who on earth would be listening in the deep night time hours, but remarkably there was an audience and we would regularly bump into people who spoke about this commentary with fondness.

Blog Post
Do coincidences and miracles exist on a single spectrum? If so, where on that spectrum does the following incident sit?

We're struggling to find out what's going on with Rhubarb Radio. Our web-streaming isn't working and we need it for tomorrow. A call goes out via social media for help. The excellent Chris Unitt calls up offering assistance. Whilst talking to Chris our doorbell goes, it's the guy sent by Flatpack Festival to pick up Women & Theatre's furniture for their festival hub. I wave him in and keep talking to Chris. The call ends I apologise for being rude "I'm trying to fix a problem". He replies, "You were talking about servers and streaming, I work with Rhubarb Radio as a technician, what's your problem?"

Fifteen minutes later our In-streamer box is reset and works perfectly. Thank you social media types. Thank you Laws of Chance / Lord of Chance – all is wonderful again.

23rd March, 2011

Tweet: 25th March 2011 10:12 Chris says "To the commentators… Sweet dreams… Mine were odd last night; I dreamt of a cat doing a hand brake turn on a quadbike while the bus 22 stopped by tikka tikka to get some cash… Disturbing…"

The Commentators Call: The World Gurning Championships
Craig Stephens and James Yarker
Sound Engineer: Simon Hanson
Commissioned by AND Festival (2011)

We knew about the World Gurning Championships, it had appeared on the Children's television programme *Blue Peter* when we were kids. Essentially it's an inverse beauty contest. Competitors take the stage, place their heads through a dray horse's halter, pull the most grotesque face they can manage and a team of judges select the winner. It's the kind of eccentric local tradition that is perfect for off-beat news stories and colour pieces for magazine format television shows - such as *Blue Peter*. The competition takes place in Egremont's Town Hall as the grand finale of the town's annual Crab and Sports Fair, attracting international media and a few curious tourists.

In 2011 a group called Abandon Normal Devices (AND) were planning to contribute to Crab and Sports Fair festivities with a programme of short films, artists' stalls on the main street, artists as competitors in events, plus a Pig Bladder Football Match and a contribution to the awards ceremony. Harun and Laura from Fierce heard about these plans and kindly introduced AND to The Commentators and hence the duo got their most prestigious booking to date.

We were fretful about this gig on at least a couple of levels. This was to be The Commentators' first venture into outside broadcasting and first proper public appearance. Webcasting from a field in Cumbria sounded technically challenging and we were unsure how local residents would take to being commentated upon by a couple of artists in sheepskin coats.

AND had the technical challenge well under control by booking sound engineer Simon Hanson, who was tethered to us all day with a ton of kit and a smart phone.

We tried to keep a low key presence when commentating and no one seemed bothered by us either around town or down at the sports field. We attended the pipe smoking contest on Friday night as research. On Saturday we commentated on greasy pole climbing, a street race and a parade including apples being thrown from a cart. Down on the field, in the afternoon, we commentated on Cumberland & Westmorland wrestling, wheelbarrow races, a children's pet competition, the pig's bladder football match, a beagle display, ferret racing and the Jez Avery Stunt Show.

By 9pm things were getting lively in the Town Hall as a packed crowd waited for the Junior, Women's and Open categories of the Gurning competition. Our plan was to stay inconspicuous at the back of the hall, but it turned out this was where the bar was set up and we were squarely in people's way, so we moved to the right hand side of the hall where we had seen a couple of television cameras set up. Having established ourselves in this advanced position we were beckoned further forward by a friendly guy who seemed to be part of the organising team and in charge of security. He installed us right at the front, almost under the stage and with a thumb up or down gave us tips on which competitors to look out for. He also explained that the sometimes tense relationship between the locals and the international media circus, came from a condescension brought by the journalists, as if they were on an anthropological field trip, rather than witnessing a community having a laugh and a party. In this context *The Commentators* were a good fit this guy at least at loved it. For our part we started getting genuinely carried away, in the uproar of the hall we found ourselves shouting, with almost no sense of irony, lines such as "We are just seconds away from discovering who is to be crowned Gurning Champion of the World 2011, live and exclusive, only on this station, do not go away!"

The Commentators Call: Billesley Primary Sports Day
Graeme Rose and Craig Stephens
With help from Evie Boulstridge and James Yarker
(2013)

The Commentators had a fallow year in 2012 but in 2013 they were back with a bang at another major sporting event, the Billesley Primary School sports day.

We had recently started working with the school to see what could happen if we acted as 'artists in residence'. We were looking for ways to help the school with their ambitions to move from 'special measures' status to become an 'outstanding' school. We thought The Commentators would add a bit of extra excitement to Sports Day and so took a portable PA system down to Moseley Rugby Club's training ground with us. When the athletes arrived they were greeted by the 2012 Olympic Fanfare and the full commentary treatment complete with post-event interviews.

It was a sunny afternoon; students, parents and teachers loved sports day and The Commentators got to commentate on all the classic events that are missing from the Olympics: egg and spoon races, sack races, three legged races and the obstacle course.

The Commentators Call:
The opening of the Library of Birmingham
Craig Stephens and James Yarker
Sound Engineer: Jon Ward
Thanks to Canstream
Commissioned by Capsule for Library of Birmingham (2013)

Connoisseurs of The Commentators will recall that their first appearance was at a twenty four hour Scalextric race made possible by Stan's Cafe moving into a new rehearsal space. This move was prompted by the company's previous space being knocked down to make way for a library. Although that library was never built and the site became a field, a different library was eventually built in a different place, on the other side of Birmingham's City Centre, on Centenary Square, attached to Birmingham Repertory Theatre. As the opening of this new Library of Birmingham drew close local arts pioneers Capsule won the contract to programme the venue's opening season of arts activity. They kindly asked The Commentators to share this notable civic event with listeners around the world.

Capsule had also commissioned Studio Myerscough to build a wonderfully colourful pavilion for the new library's grey foyer space and our commentary table was to be set up in there, facing the main revolving doors and beside the main escalators, rising up to the reference library and the slope down to the lending libraries. We could see everyone entering and leaving the building and for the first time since *24 Hour Scalextric* our commentary was to be both streamed online and heard live over speakers in the venue, where the unwitting audience would also find themselves cast as performers.

Blog Post
As I type, the red carpet is being positioned outside the new Library of Birmingham. The Commentators are installed behind their beaten up table opposite the shiny new revolving doors which will admit guests to tonight's VIP reception. The event runs 18:30 – 20:30, commentary will start at 18:00 and run from 10:00 on Tuesday morning for the public opening at 11:30. The link to listen to live streamed commentary follows, if it shows an error message this should just mean you have tried to tune in outside broadcast hours, please try again later. Listen to The Commentators Live from the Library of Birmingham here.

2nd September, 2013

As a major civic function the library's opening event was attended by a huge array of local notables all of whom were subject to The Commentator's 'red carpet' commentary. The following morning an eager and inquisitive public came streaming into the building. We had long fun days, some people ignored us, some hurried past to avoid us and some played up to us courting commentary like kids in front of a distorting mirror, experimenting to see the reactions to their actions.

Of course some people thought we were idiots and for a brief while I became painfully aware that I was an idiot.

Blog Post

I'm really pleased to learn that Malala Yousafzai has become a Nobel Laurette. She is an extraordinary person. The thing I find easy to forget is that she was extraordinary before she was shot by the Taliban. She was shot because she was extraordinary and her response to the shooting merely confirmed how extraordinary she is. By shooting Malala the Taliban have empowered her.

Coincidence combined with expertise led Malala to be brought to Birmingham for her treatment. In a breathtakingly smart move Edgbaston High School for Girls, just down the road from us, offered to help with the next stage of her education and last year Malala was the guest of honour opening the Library of Birmingham.

Malala performing this opening was a humbling and deeply uncomfortable experience for me. The Commentators had been commissioned to commentate on the library's first three days of operation. We were having tremendous fun doing our ridiculous over-keen thing, giving an alternative comedic slant to events. Then I found myself outside, within the press cordon, clutching a radio microphone commentating on Malala giving her deeply moving speech, unveiling the sign and – actually I don't think she cut a ribbon but maybe she did. I was commentating on this extraordinary girl being honoured in this special way and there was no way my commentator character could exist in the same realm as her. So I became just a middle aged man, in a sheepskin coat, pretending to be a sports commentator thinking "this is no way to earn a living".

It was a relief to learn that my radio mic signal had not made it through the library's toughened glass and Craig had covered the whole thing from a much worse vantage point.

Being one of The Commentators is still a ridiculous way to earn a living, so its fortunate that they don't meet the likes of Malala very often, but then, who does?

11th October, 2014

The Commentators Call: Children In Need
Craig Stephens and James Yarker
Sound Engineer: Peter Maxwell Dixon
(2013)

Blog post
Exciting news! In a rare development for The Commentators their phones rang today., in an even rarer development it turned out to be their agent. Astonishingly, she had received a call from the BBC asking after their availability this Friday. Being a good agent she replied that this would "depend on some factors" and that she "could move a few things around" and basically "yes they are" (they could be called off the golf course and out of the potting shed).

After all these years the BBC were calling again and not 'just' BBC Midlands but 'the network', BBC 1, Live Television, the biggest audience since they last did the FA Cup Final, which was back in the days when people watched the FA Cup Final. Admittedly it is just going to be 20 seconds worth, but it means their faces (and voices) will be back in the public eye (and ear). It is for Children In Need and so there isn't actually a fee attached to the work but their agent has assured them this is a good deal and that she is kindly also prepared waive her cut as it is for such a good cause.

Listen to The Commentators from Children In Need at the Library of Birmingham 18:00 – 22:00 on Friday on this website and live on BBC 1 for twenty seconds in the final hour – unless someone over runs or someone more interesting becomes available.

13th November, 2013

Following our residency at the Library of Birmingham over its opening weekend, we were invited back to the venue as part of that year's Children In Need fundraising event. We streamed live from the venue and made a fleeting on-screen appearance. It was instructive to be inside the event, seeing the true level of artifice involved. As a viewer there is always something deeply unconvincing about the jollity of those events and our experience in front of the camera confirmed that the jollity is entirely fabricated. In no sense are the cameras 'popping in to report on a party', there is no party, at the Library Of Birmingham on that day it was 100% television show and 0% party. Craig, the consummate actor and improviser, was smooth in front of the camera. I was stitched up by the interviewer, who stole my rehearsal answer as part of his on-air, question leaving me very little to say but I thought I'd put on a brave face. Watching at home my wife she could see a bitter hatred of it all burning in my eyes. Ah well, it's all for charity isn't it!

The Commentators Call: BE Festival Awards Ceremony
Craig Stephens and James Yarker
Master of Ceremonies: Graeme Rose
(2014)

New commissions work for The Commentators like Case Law, helping us define the rules around what they can and can't do. When BE Festival asked The Commentators to host their end of festival awards ceremony this felt problematic as commentators are never supposed to be centre stage. In our imagining of them they only exist in relation to the event they are commentating on, they are no substantial enough as characters to exist on their own.

We resolved this difficulty by inviting Graeme Rose to act as Master of Ceremonies. He could work through the mechanics of announcing awards while also leaving space for The Commentators to be heard commentating on him, the nominees, audience and winners. The improvisation became three way.

Graeme's prior experience as one of The Commentators meant it all worked smoothly; this playful approach was in keeping with the experimental and informal atmosphere of the BE Festival.

The Commentators Call: Moseley Folk Festival
Craig Stephens and James Yarker
Technical help: Jon Ward
Commissioned by Moseley Folk Festival (2014)

We had been attending the excellent Moseley Folk festival as audience members for a number of years before receiving the invitation to add commentary to the event. Bell wire strung between trees linked our amplifier to domestic speakers in plastic bags fixed in locations around the festival site where music wouldn't drown us out. We were heard at the entrance gate, at the toilets, beside the food concessions and near the bar. Our requirements for a radio microphone with talk-back facility were added to the festival's technical hire and long time Stan's Cafe Associate Artist, Jon Ward plugged us up, monitored levels, recorded our ramblings and in lieu of live streaming, posted edited 'highlights' to a SoundCloud account. We were positioned in a scaffold access tower at the top of the festival's main field looking down over the crowd at the Main and subsidiary Lunar stages. We were ready to go.

Blog Post
Terrifyingly someone has slipped The Commentators Access All Areas wristbands for the Moseley Folk Festival, which means they can now bring their loyal listeners exclusive coverage from everywhere and anywhere. Tonight Johnny Marr was able to suit-up un-commentated upon backstage but tomorrow night will Richard Thompson be so lucky? On Saturday will The Waterboys escape having their entire rider inventoried over the airwaves?

Visit this website regularly over the weekend for podcasts bringing you the 'Almost Live' experience of Moseley Folk. If you are on-site over the weekend, seek out any one of nine listening posts to find out exactly what's going on where you are and in areas not everyone can access.

29th August, 2014

We had to learn how The Commentators worked in this new setting and it took a little trial and error.

Blog Post
The Commentators were much better on Sunday than they were on Saturday. After that first day we reflected on what went well and what could have gone better. As each outing for The Commentators is a new setting we have to answer the question as to how it works in that setting. Sometimes that can be established in advance; at the BE Festival we made a plan and executed it. Sometimes we have to learn from experience.

At the folk festival the first day informed the second. We decided we needed to spend a lot more time out and about with the roving microphone to get into the detail of festival activity as options were too limited from our brilliant gantry position. The security guards asked for a 'shout out' so this helped us recognise that many people enjoyed hearing themselves being commentated on, so we determined to do more of that. We remembered enjoying the elements where the sporting lens was held up to the event and when fictions and speculations were conjured up and allowed to run. We resolved to do more of these.

Sunday started with a high energy and didn't let up much for the full eight hours, much better, fun to do and encouraging enough to suggest we look for more outings in similar settings.

To Gerv and Carl – who programme the festival – in the words of failed candidates on *The Apprentice* "thank you for the opportunity".

1st September, 2014

The Commentators Call:
The Public Theater Foyer, New York City
Craig Stephens and Graeme Rose
Commissioned by Under The Radar (2015)

Blog Post

Tomorrow The Commentators return. This time they are 'stateside' for their first American engagement since the heady days of the original New York Cosmos – Pele, Beckenbauer et al. On Friday they will bringing eager listeners all the comings, goings and lingerings in the Foyer of The Public Theater, Manhattan. Due to the time difference UK listeners will have to tune in between 23:30 and 03:30 GMT to catch the action live as it happens (the link will be on this homepage).

With members of Stan's Cafe including Craig and Graeme in New York to perform The Cardinals it made sense for The Commentators to tag along as well for a performance in the Foyer of the famous Public Theater. Here they mostly described people queueing to get into shows but there is a proud American tradition of entertaining queues and a sports mad media savvy New York public was an appreciative audience for our very British style of sports broadcasting.

The time lag made it a particularly exciting experience to tune in for at home, as if it were World Championship Boxing from Madison Square Garden.

15th January, 2015

The Commentators Call:
The Lunar Festival, Tanworth-in-Arden
Craig Stephens and James Yarker
Technical help: Jon Ward with Georgiana Mihai
Commissioned by Lunar Festival Festival (2015)

The Lunar Festival is Moseley Folk's sister festival, the music is a bit more rocky, the site is larger and it offers overnight camping. The larger festival site meant The Commentators didn't feel so central to proceedings but this space allowed us to position speakers in areas where people could choose to sit near them listening to us and acts on the main stage at the same time. This meant we could watch people's reaction to our commentary and see what was hitting home.

We had a beautifully crafted commentary box and watched a lot of workshop activities including slack lining and circus skills.

The Commentators Call: Moseley Folk Festival
Craig Stephens and James Yarker
Technical help: Jon Ward
Commissioned by Moseley Folk Festival (2015)

It was very encouraging to be invited back to the Moseley Folk festival for a second time. We must have been doing something right.

Junior Commentators West Bromwich 2016

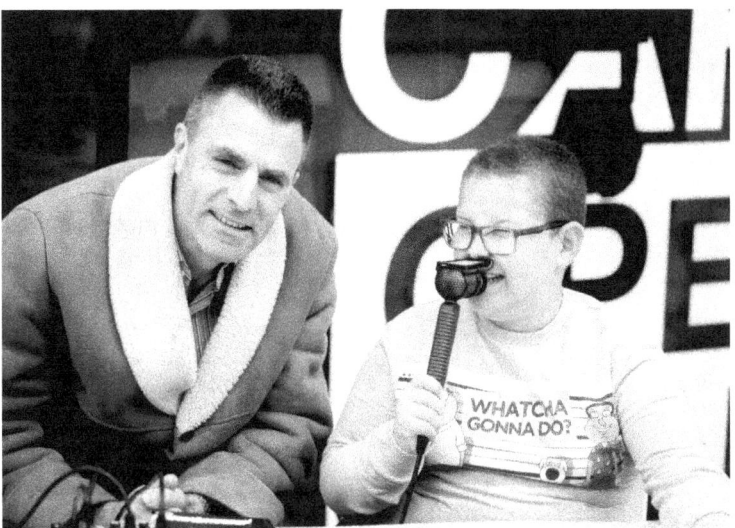

For years primary school students had been commentating on Scalextric races we were staging in their schools, now a commission from Creative Black Country invited us to take some Junior Commentators out on to the streets.

Blog
On Saturday a team of apprentice commentators from the Lyng Media Club take to the streets of West Bromwich as part of the Sandwell Arts Festival. A team of twelve young people aged between 5 and 12 will be on the streets between 12:00 – 15:00 reporting on all the goings on in the town centre during festival time.

We have had two training sessions. The group already knew about commentators, a bit from football, but more enthusiastically from Wrestle Mania. This was a start, but how to train them in the dark arts of 'street commentary' was a significant challenge.

On Tuesday we tried lots of different speaking games and description challenges before I cracked open the dominoes. With eight members of the group setting up dominoes and four commentating of their efforts everyone was kept busy and on task in rotation. We took in some fresh air to practice commentating in the street before wrapping up by setting out a Scalextric loop and commentating on a series of one minute races.

On Thursday we did much the same session but increased the level of difficulty and introduced microphones and a mixing desk to proceedings. They were all better than they were on Tuesday and delivered some lovely moments. Everyone seems to have enjoyed their training sessions but I'm not sure how much closer they are to being ready for tomorrow.

Pina Bausch's Kontakthof is performed by three casts: the professional Wuppertal Dance company, a team of elderly amateur ballroom dancers and a youth cast. It was fascinating and poignant seeing the senior version in Hannover years ago, imaging the same material embodied by its original cast. The West Bromwich scenario is different, we have very young cast improvising their own material. It remains to be seen how skilled the cast can be in their execution and how robust the idea is to work if the execution isn't very skilled. On the flip-side it remains to be seen what the cast's youth will bring to the show that Craig and I, as haggard old grown ups, can't hope to emulate.

Putting shows under stress is a useful way to learn about them and of course let's not forget that giving the young people a great experience, extra confidence and some new skills is the least we hope to achieve and reason enough to be doing this. Thanks to Creative Black Country for the commission.

12th August, 2016

Sat at a table outside the local arts centre with speakers and their lip microphones the junior commentators did well. I sat beside them in a supporting role, providing continuity. Most of the team were brave enough to take a turn and some were irrepressible. Passers by were encouraging about their efforts and the event had an uplifting 'feel good' quality to it.

The Commentators Call: Jewellery Quarter Festival 2017
Craig Stephens and Jack Trow
Commissioned by Jewellery Quarter BID

A feature of our coverage of the Moseley Folk Festival was Craig's perambulations around the site with a radio microphone. Initially the idea of this was to bring 'listeners at home' close-up reports of festival happenings, yet it quickly became clear that, as we experienced in the Library of Birmingham, many people enjoy being the subject of commentary. Often members of the public would act up for the commentator, with Craig responding to these responses and prompting fresh action, a loose improvisation would follow. This interaction between performer and public is the essence of a strand of walkabout street theatre and could, in theory, operate effectively on its own independent of any other commentary infrastructure.

This theory was to be tested out when The Commentators were invited to cover the Jewellery Quarter Festival in Birmingham's most attractive business district. For this gig The Commentators operated with their microphones plugged directly into a busker's battery powered mobile speaker. There was no web-streaming, no fixed speakers and no base. It turned out to be a liberating experience and new angle for The Commentators.

The Commentators Call: Moseley Folk Festival
Craig Stephens and James Yarker
Technical help: Jon Ward
Commissioned by Moseley Folk Festival (2017)

After a year's break to accommodate other Stan's Cafe commitments The Commentators were back, refreshed, at Moseley Folk Festival and touched by the welcome they got from audiences who professed to have missed them in 2016.

The Commentators Call: The Bull Ring Open Market
Craig Stephens and Graeme Rose
Technical help: Peter Maxwell-Dixon
Commissioned by Birmingham Weekender (2017)

Blog Post

On Saturday 23rd, as part of Birmingham's Weekender event The Commentators are streaming live radio commentary from the Bull Ring Open Market. I was very excited about this opportunity until I realised that a family commitment 50 years in the making means I have to relinquish my seat, lip mic and sheepskin coat to Graeme; my daughter is overcome with relief.

I love the Bull Ring markets, note not Bullring – the omnivorous private mall, but the set of three council run markets just south of the bland behemoth. The Indoor Market majors on fish and meat with a scattering of other stalls. The Rag Market focuses on fabrics, clothes, shoes and hardware. The Open Market is outdoors and it is principally populated by fruit and vegetable stalls. I'm a fan of all three but the Open Market is may favourite, it's more raw.

In 1991 I was time rich and money poor, I lived on Ombersley Road and would walk a mile and half to the market, buy as much fruit and veg as it was possible to carry and stagger home, the bunched up plastic carrier bag handles cutting the blood supply to my fingers.

On my first visit I wandered around trying to decide which stall should have my first custom and realised it had to be the man in the vest, bouncing around, bubbling over with banter, pumping out energy. I bought 10lb of potatoes for £1 from Carl Seigel and remained his customer for the next twenty years.

Carl piled good quality vegetables high and sold them cheaply, he was consistently cheery, had great repartee and built relationships with his customers, remembering their stories and sharing fragments of his own live. Occasionally you would see someone hard up being slipped a free bag of veg.

Over the years Carl's stall changed with the evolution of the market; it moved when the 60's version of the market was demolished to make way for Bulling. Later the vegetables started to arrive trimmed and scrubbed clean of mud. His bags ceased to be branded by whatever bankrupt firm had sold its bag stock off and became the homogenous blue that the rest of the market used. Once strictly a root vegetable man, Carl started stocking broccoli and later even vine tomatoes and ultimately even, occasionally, mangos. Unable to stem the march of 'progress' he eventually laid out a few £1 a bowl deals. Carl got a bit ill but bounced back, he started wearing a weightlifter's belt for back support, always whip thin he started to look gaunt and one day he wasn't there. His stall was there, with its familiar "Jolly Nice" labels still in his handwriting but he wasn't behind the stall, which was now being run by one of his former assistants. Carl had retired and I'd never got the chance to congratulate him and thank him.

Eamon sells me most of my fresh fruit. He likes fishing, has had two replacement knees and always enquires after Eve who he's known since she was born. John, with his soft fingers, sells free range eggs £1 for six. Shopping at the market reminds me of shopping with my Grandmother in Rye in the mid-seventies, going to a different shop for each class of goods and having conversations with each shopkeeper as she went.

Within these steady relationships I like the unpredictability of the market. What exotic goods will have flooded the stalls this week? What will be mysteriously 'out of season' and unavailable? What eccentric people will be around? What will the banter between the stall holders be today? What street evangelists will be shouting, what buskers playing, what fortunes with the Gypsy in her caravan tell?

Supermarkets ensure eating healthily is crippling expensive, in the Open Markets it's cheap. From the supermarkets the fruit is rarely ripe, from the Open Markets the cheapest food is so ripe you have to eat it as fast as you can and turn the rest into soup. This is one of the few places in Birmingham where the rich and poor push past each other, rub shoulders and queue together. It's a real place and I love it.

Craig and Graeme will have no trouble finding enough action to commentate on.
23rd September, 2017

Indeed they didn't, they had a stall of their own and did a healthy trade in quips and observations with the engaged and engaging stall holders and their customers.

The Commentators Call: Moseley Folk Festival
Craig Stephens and James Yarker
Technical help: Peter Maxwell-Dixon with Ryan Knight
Commissioned by Moseley Folk Festival (2018)

Blog post
We are spending this weekend at Moseley Folk Festival performing as The Commentators, spinning out a *Test Match Special* style radio sports commentary over folk proceedings for seven hours at a stretch, Saturday and Sunday 11:00 – 18:00. Our innovation for this year is that the whole thing can be heard live online around the festival site, at home, wherever you can connect to the internet.

Arty types might call The Commentators 'long form improvisation', less arty types might call it 'having a laugh' and less enlightened types certainly call it 'droning on'. We've been performing The Commentators in various non or almost sporting settings since 2009. This is our fourth time at this festival and I'm amazed that they keep asking us back; I cling to the fact that they do when beset by self-doubt with hours left to go each day.

It's easiest to commentate imagining people are listening in an imaginary world. The idea that actual people yards away in this actual world are actually listening is always deeply concerning. To keep us on track we have a number of unwritten rules and guidelines concerning.

The Commentators they:
- are endlessly enthusiastic and optimistic.
- are interested in everything.
- have hypotheses and speculate.
- are never nasty, cruel or unpleasant.
- can be skeptical and are often cautious.
- are experts but never on the subject they are discussing.
- understand sport and read most of life as sport.
- always speak to 'listeners at home'.
- rarely give even hints of their lives beyond this moment.
- are never trying to be funny.

It would drive us crazy performing as The Commentators too much but fortunately we have other things on. This coming week we're in Saltley Academy working on the latest edition of *The Steps Series* which in an installation we've been reinventing since 2008. Next week we're in Madrid with *Of All The People In All The World*, a performance we first made in 2003. Last week we revived our first hit theatre show *It's Your Film* which we made in 1998 and to balance out all these revivals and reinventions, on 17th September we start rehearsing a brand new theatre show, *The Capital* which will open on 24th October at The REP in Birmingham, before going on tour..

Until any of that we have a whole weekend of minutia to keep the listening public up to date with. Please tune in before we drop out.

31st August, 2018

The Commentators Call: The Nutcracker
Craig Stephens and James Yarker
Technical help: Peter Maxwell-Dixon
In collaboration with Birmingham Royal Ballet (2018)

Blog Post
It's taken a few years to finally sort out but at last we are proud to announce that this Thursday, 29th November from 19:00 GMT The Commentators will be bringing you live and exclusive radio commentary of Birmingham Royal Ballet's performance of *The Nutcracker*. Coverage will be streamed live from this website and there will be no 'listen again' facility so make sure are near a computer on Thursday to hear 'Ballet on the Radio'.

We approached BRB director David Bintley with our proposal a number of years ago. There had been some scepticism about my chances of persuading this esteemed choreographer to let our washed up sports radio commentators loose on one of his cherished company's productions, but as soon as I saw an Aston Villa mug on his desk I knew it would be a breeze and so it proved, no persuasion was necessary. David immediately understood the idea and seemed delighted by it, we agreed it had to happen.

The Nutcracker has been chosen as, being one of the world's most famous ballets, a proportion of the audience will be able to picture it in their minds-eye and compare that image with The Commentator's description of it. Being such a canonical work *The Nutcracker* is a robust enough cultural object to survive further processing, even if this an audio only version.

Back in June we had a test commentary during a piano rehearsal of *Romeo and Juliet*. We set up in the Hippodrome's Royal Box, using some perspex sound baffles to keep us from distracting audience members seated nearby. The Royal Box has an ante-room which, conveniently, is kitted out with a ethernet socket. Streaming our commentary out over the internet wasn't a problem, no one could hear us in the auditorium, a few admin details had to be sorted out and we're ready to go on Thursday. This is David Bintley's last season at BRB so Thursday will probably be a one-off, we hope you can tune in.

26th November, 2018

This gig fulfilled a long held ambition. Behind the scenes there was a ludicrous amount of negotiating over whether the musicians playing Tchaikovsky's score would be audible enough in the background of our commentary to be entitled to a bonus payment. Ultimately it was agreed that they would be and this extra sum was found by Birmingham Royal Ballet. These rights also placed restrictions on how much of our recording could be shared as a public archive, however, our main focus was the live broadcast, which was excellent fun and a great new challenge for The Commentators.

The athleticism involved in Ballet provided a good link with the putative sporting heritage of The Commentators and David Bintley showed what a great sport he is by visiting the commentary box for a 'half time' interview. He was quizzed on team selection, the first half performance, injury worries, home advantage and video reviews. He answered these questions with great eloquence and good humour.

The Commentators Call:
Birmingham Young Professional Of The Year Awards
Jack Trow and James Yarker
Technical help: Peter Maxwell-Dixon
Commissioned by Birmingham Future (2019)

In contrast to the BE Festival Awards, to which The Commentators brought their own master or ceremonies, at the Birmingham Young Professional Of The Year Awards that role was already taken and The Commentators were operating where they feel comfortable, on the fringes of the action.

The plan was simple, to provide a genuine service to family and friends of nominees, allowing them to hear in real time if their loved ones had won an award, plus adding some roaming on-site entertainment around the tables, akin to, but entirely different from, the service close-up magicians provide.

The Commentators did a decent job but things never took off. The award's organising committee were fantastic and keen to disrupt the stale award show formula with some commentary but ultimately these events are so powerfully formulaic that they strongly resist disruption. Guests couldn't really work out who we were or why we were there. It was very difficult for The Commentators to chisel out space in this noisy, uniformly glitzy corporate environment and this uniformity and strictly regulated activity made the event very challenging to describe in an interesting way for an extended time. A rare misfire for The Commentators but a good change to learn how they work.

The Commentators Call: Jewellery Quarter Festival
Craig Stephens and James Yarker
(2019)

This was an enjoyable repeat gig in our home quadrant of our home town. There was commentary on a circus theatre troupe, home made compressed air rocket test firings and a lot of coverage of a miniature steam train service.

The Commentators Call: Moseley Folk Festival
Craig Stephens and James Yarker
Technical help: Peter Maxwell-Dixon with Ryan Knight
Commissioned by Moseley Folk Festival (2019)

We had been very happy with our new 2018 location, being lower down had made us more visible to the crowd and made interaction with people much easier. We finished that year with an understanding of how we could approach the following year to make the most of this position. However the next year promoter Carl had had a fresh idea.

For 2019 our commentary position was moved to the bottom of the main field alongside the Main Stage and Lunar Stage facing back towards our previous commentary position. Now we could see audience's faces and they could clearly see us, we were now a miniature third stage framed in cut out hardboard as if we were sitting inside a huge old fashioned television set.

This new position meant we couldn't see anything that was happening on the Lunar Stage next to us and could only see the very front section of the Main Stage. Although this was a massive inconvenience, massive inconveniences suit The Commentators. We were now more obviously a notable feature of the festival and our new position allowed us to be plugged into the main PA system, so at a pre-determined moment our output 'accidentally' started to come through the festival's main speakers, much to our faux horror (and genuine terror).

This gig was also the first after we had retired the collection of old domestic speakers we had repurposed years ago for this job they were almost entirely unsuited for. Now we had bought proper fairground / gymkhana / summer fete waterproof public address speakers. Back stage Peter Maxwell-Dixon came up trumps with a set of old radios he had rewired to work as speakers so they could carry The Commentators' commentary to the artists' bar backstage.

After initial reservations about our new location we enjoyed this weekend very much.

Film On The Radio with The Commentators
Craig Stephens and James Yarker
(2020)

In March 2020 a virus pandemic closed theatres, cinemas and sporting venues around the world. Millions of people were told to stay at home and cease direct interactions with each other. Humanitarians to a fault, The Commentators answered the call for public service in restoring morale and set up their own radio show.

The premise of *Film On The Radio with The Commentators* was extremely simple. The Commentators provide a moment by moment radio commentary on a selection of Hollywood's most popular films. Broadcast as live and available afterwards as podcasts, these audio descriptions were made without The Commentators having any prior knowledge of the film, its plot or cast. Neither The Commentators, nor the audience at home could hear any of the film's soundtrack.

Although the name of the film described was never made public once identified, knowledgable listeners were able to source the film and synch the commentary to visuals for a new take on an old and familiar movie.

This process has antecedents in numerous previous Stan's Cafe productions. *Come Together* (2008) is a ten minute long theatre show performed in synch with an unheard recording of Primal Scream's album track of the same name. *Twilightofthefreakingods* (2013) has the narrative of Götterdämerung performed to the timings but not the sound of Georg Solti's Vienna Philharmonic recording of Wagner's opera. In *A Translation Of Shadows* (2015) a narrator, in the old Japanese Benshi tradition, explains what is happening in a silent film. In *I See With My Eyes Closed* (2010) a live audience hears what's going on in the minds of two audience members sat in their midst watching a performance by Birmingham Contemporary Music Group. There is so much that interests us in the interaction between art and its audience, how information is encoded, decoded and interpreted according to different people's experiences and thought processes, we keep returning to explore this engagement from fresh angles.

The Future of The Commentators.

We hope that The commentators will continue to be invited to their favourite arenas, such as Moseley Folk Festival and the Jewellery Quarter Festival, but equally we hope that they will continue to be placed in new contexts to respond to new challenges and recognise new ways of looking at the world.

Reflections On The Commentators

So what?
Rather than being some carefully conceived and precisely executed project, *The Commentators* has evolved and adapted to circumstances and whilst we have reflected on the project we have never subjected it to any systematic interrogation. Until now...

Life as Sport
After the first performance we invented a broad back-story for The Commentators. "They were once fully fledged, successful sports commentators (hence they dress like the iconic John Motson), but now they have fallen on hard times, they must accept any commentary job that comes along".

So far their commissions have split roughly into two strands, those which are very low grade sports commentaries and those which aren't sports commentaries at all. In the sporting category we have slot cars, not Grand Prix; a crowd watching World Cup football, not World Cup football; yes athletics, but primary school athletics, none of whose events resembled any Olympic event; even the Sports Fair contained mostly egg throwing, ferret racing and face pulling (Gurning). Northumberland Wrestling in Egremont was as genuine and high profile a sport as The Commentators have commentated on since we've known them. Of course because they are sports commentators there is usually a sporting inflection to their commentary even on those occasions where there isn't even 'nearly sport' around: a gallery opening, a library opening, a mostly deserted street in the night.

The Rules
A few rules have emerged through the commentary. They are always optimistic and never cynical and everything is equally fascinating (though occasionally only to one of them - usually James).

The place of the audience varies, lying on a spectrum from

Broad Street, where The Commentators were entirely invisible and with their only audience distant and tuned in on-line, through the football crowd and Egremont public, who could see but not hear the commentators, whilst in the openings and Scalextric, audiences listened both live and on-line. At the sports day, whist the commentators spoke as if they were broadcasting to the world, technical constraints (which as with most technical constraints were actually budgetary constraints) prevented a webcast.

In the Library of Birmingham The Commentators worked from a pavilion in the Library's entrance hall. Speakers relayed their commentary beyond the pavilion so it could be heard by the people being commentated upon. A fascinating element of this experience was to watch people's dawning realisation that they were the subject of the commentary and watching their response to this, which included embarrassed acknowledgement, feigned ignorance, occasional irritation but often great good humour and often acting up for the commentary. There were many who whilst not being commentated upon attempted to do something which would provoke us to mention them.

The commentary is all improvised. Occasionally some preparation has been done to provide some materials to draw upon, but this is rare, mostly done by Craig and a script is never written. Some ideas are picked up but fizzle out, some ideas are run with and can be referred back to, becoming strands or themes. The Library of Birmingham generated its own structure, with each commentator taking one major walk around each day with shared time at the table in between.

At the Library of Birmingham we had to be careful to appear to only ever be commentating for listeners at home when in fact much of what we were saying was for those present at the library.

Thanks to the mighty Jon Ward a series of 'highlight' recordings are being made available online for people to catch up on The

Commentators at the Library of Birmingham. You are welcome to listen to them but rather like TV highlights of a five day test match, these recordings rather miss the point.

The point of The Commentators isn't the highlights. The point is the monstrous duration. Eight hours unbroken commentary of something that isn't conventionally interesting. In this sense the twelve hours through the night at not quite Broad Street was the paradigm commentary.

Whilst performing *The Commentators* it is difficult to think about anything other than "what's the other person saying now and what am I going to say next?" That's the point of it in many ways, what do you say next? You set yourselves the task of commentating on something that appears to be uninteresting and you have committed to do it for a very long time, what the hell do you say next? When you finish performing and reflect on the event then the interesting questions start cropping up.

Why can't you interview people?
Because it doesn't work.

Why doesn't it work?
Because the interviewee is placed in an impossible position, they are a real person being asked a question by a fictional commentator, how should they respond? Somehow this question and answer moment shorts out the fiction, the interviewee needs to be in role as well. The exception was David Bintley, who was in on the joke and understood his role when interviewed at 'half time' during Birmigham Royal Ballet's performance of *The Nutcracker*.

You are allowed to hint at a back-story (Craig's garage filled with sports reference books and biographies which could do with the same motorised racking system employed by Library of Birmingham). It feels best only to hint at hinterland, rather than getting caught up in a weaving too elaborate a fiction in that territory, the less that's said the more room there is for audiences to project into the gaps.

We have slightly different approaches. Craig is very 'straight down the line', more disciplined, more funny. I tend to allow myself a longer leash, to go off on more speculative journeys of wild speculation, over-detailed description, wanderings into awkward cul-de-sacs that cannot be reversed out of, all safe in the knowledge that Craig, at some point, will cut in with "Anyway, back to...". As a result, Craig's commentary is very smooth, whilst occasionally I feel I've overdone something or forced a gag a bit too hard.

One of the keys is that The Commentators aren't supposed to be funny. Their task is absurd, so fundamentally, where there is humour it should stem from that, the absurdity of staring at an empty car park at four in the morning and finding something more to say about it.

We're often asked how we keep going, but in truth the difficulty is stopping. Once you've stopped an eight hour shift as a commentator that commentating voice has become internalised and you can't stand to be with yourself because you're driving yourself insane and if you dare speak the chances are that you'll drive your partner insane too, because you will say too much, give too much information, make an observation that really doesn't need to be made, unless, as you have been for the previous eight hours, you are contractually obliged to speak.

As boys we commentated on our own football matches or cricket matches, either aloud or internally, and when we rode our bikes we were grand prix drivers and when we walked to school we were either still racing drivers or champion walkers and possibly even doing the washing up we were competing in the washing up championships. As *24 Hour Scalextric* was a refusal to grow up, so *The Commentators* draws on our basic drive to see sport or competition in everything.

Why do people listen for so long at a stretch?
Partly because people do just leave the radio on and don't listen for as long as the data suggests, but many people do say

they find *The Commentators* actively difficult to turn off and our Associate Artist Jon Ward, drawing on his professional experience with BBC Radio, has pinpointed why. The Commentators don't give their listeners permission to turn off. There are no breaks in the commentary and no joins. Jon notes that professional broadcasters hate their programs being interrupted by the news, sport or weather as each of these breaks in the programme's flow are possible excuses for audiences to leave. The Commentators never cut to anything else, they are are always in mid-flow so it would always be rude to turn them off and to turn off would always be to miss the end of something that hasn't finished.

There are probably hints of surveillance about T*he Commentators*, we are CCTV for the radio; the eyes that don't blink broadcasting for the ears that don't close.

We have a number of unfulfilled commentary ambitions, but there is still time, The Commentators may not be prolific but they are a long way from retirement.

James Yarker, September 2013 tweaked in 2020

Tuning Out With Radio Z

This show was the convergence of many ideas and interests.

Some time, perhaps in 2007, I had attended my first conference at which a message board was projected on a screen behind the speaker, enabling audience members to back up the speaker's ideas, to add references, to contradict, undermine them or even converse about something else entirely. It seemed like a terrifying prospect for any speaker and a ludicrous distraction, but an intriguing theatrical device.

In 2008 much of the world suffered a major financial crisis. In 2009 we investigated staging a Brecht play in our new venue. Our plan was to respond to the financial crisis and explore an audience critiquing a show mid-show. Unfortunately we couldn't find a Brecht play that served our purposes and instead make our own fake Brecht show, *The Just Price Of Flowers*. That play didn't suit our message board idea, which remained unstarted business.

As mentioned earlier in this book, our new venue led to us to stage a twenty four hour Scalextric race. From this production we grew interested in the different audience experiences listening to an event live via internet radio and attending the event. This gulf felt worth exploring further.

Our original plans for *Lurid and Insane* (2001) set the show in a radio station just after a revolution. That idea evolved into a band performing a concert and our commissioning the theatre company Hamfisted! to create and broadcast *People's Radio Freedom* as preamble to the show. One of my favourite theatre experiences was being in a car driving to see *Lurid and Insane* while tuned into the show's one radio station.

The glue that stuck these tentative ideas together was the realisation that some of my favourite moments of theatre came in the rehearsal room. In those days a familiar devising technique for Stan's Cafe was for me to set the actors an improvisational task, start them going, sit back and see what they could make happen. I enjoyed watching the mechanics of them thinking and exploring together, tuning into each other's lines of exploration, dropping ideas and picking others up, perhaps getting desperate and stretching or breaking the rules. The reward, when something clicked and started working really well, was magical but audiences never saw this process or shared this magic. One of the big challenges of devising in this way is to identify this precious material, mine it and refine it so those moments doesn't need a twenty minute set up. If you are able to place these great moments one after the other you should end up with a decent show, but the audience will not share the thrill of the exploration and magic of the discovery moment. I started to think that maybe we should create an improvised show based on this rehearsal room dynamic.

So there was our constellation of ideas: an improvised show, set in a radio station, with audiences able listen at home or watch live in the theatre and both audiences in dialogue with the show via a message board projected on stage: *Tuning Out With Radio Z*

Radio Z was to be the station and the show would centre on the making of its program *Tuning Out*, hence "You're listening to *Tuning Out* with Radio Z".

Early Show Thinking

This archive document shows ideas coalescing before rehearsals started.

Listeners.
A radio station. The night shift. A DJ and his/her producer, possibly someone
D.J. = Amanda
Producer = Craig
Visitor
The audience are invited to come to the show, bringing their laptops or 3G phones.
The venue has an open broadband wireless link.
A message board is set up connected with the show that allows people to contribute to the show online.
The message board is probably not visible on stage.
But there may be a projection behind the performance which mixes night time views of he City with a screening of the message board.
The show is webcast live as radio, this is considered by the characters within the show as their real audience. No acknowledgement is made of the actual live audience. They are party to what the Radio Host and Producer say off microphone, unlike those listening on-line.
The piece has music playing throughout as part of the real/ fictional radio station. This music could either be pre-existing material replicating the sense of a real radio station or we could commission a host of musicians we know to write stuff for us, giving them a brief of the kind of thing we are after. In a way this is a more attractive option. If there were enough of this material to hand then the music could be used more as a D.J. set than a playlist.

The maximum cast list could be:
Radio Host
Producer
Early morning visitor (could easily be one of the off-stage crew doubling up)
Off-Stage:
D.J. for sounds & slides
Editor for message board texts
Lighting and slide operator (I think this role could be shared with the D.J. and Editor).
There is no pre-set. The broadcast starts before the audience is admitted to the theatre.

The show has a series of strands that, if no one contributed to the show online, would resolve themselves as a standard show. However, these strands are opened to the public to pick up-upon, embellish and make their own. The performers will be equipped with a series of strategies in order to field these contributions and weave them into the show. The duration of the show will vary with each performance and the conclusion will probably alter too. The visitor could be male or female if the D.J. and message board editors are male and female, they could also be of varying identities depending on what the most dramatic scenario appears to be given the stories which are being fed in.

The editor's role is to act as a buffer between the message board and the performers should there be an unreasonable number of contributions, their job would be to make things as simple for the performers as possible. The editor will also have the role of contributing material and prompting the performers should there be a lack of material being submitted to the message board.

The Host's console is an island, floating in the night, it possibly has Perspex screens around it, as a drummer in a recording studio would, when records are playing and the microphone is off they may come out of this to speak to the producer. The producer's desk is a separate island, or raft in the same night.

The floor should be a highly reflective surface so that the video projection has a chance of being echoed in the floor.

The lighting will be concentrated around the console, perhaps exclusively from angle-poise style lights, ideally these would be fitted with 3 colour LED systems so their colours could be changed over time in a controlled way.

The themes of the show are probably about live-ness and presence versus distance and cynicism in the media; front against integrity; fashion vs passion, that kind of thing.
There may be some excitement about someone from the outside world coming into the studio near to the end of the show.

Commissioning

In parallel with the thinking that was to become *Tuning Out With Radio Z* we had been developing the idea for a show in which three cardinals and a female muslim stage manager tell the complete history of the world in a small puppet theatre. We took both ideas to our long time partners at Warwick Arts Centre to ask them which piece they would be most keen to programme. They chose *Tuning Out With Radio Z*, which was disappointing as we knew how to make *The Cardinals* and knew that audiences would like it. We had very little idea how to make *Tuning Out With Radio Z* and thought there was a fair chance that lots of people wouldn't like it.

Our longest term partners at mac, in Birmingham, were due to reopen their venue following a major rebuild and they thought *Tuning Out With Radio Z* sounded like the kind of ambitious, no holds barred show that would work well as a commission for their first week back. Knowing a venue is waiting for our show is all the fuel we need and now we have two, enough to build a tour around. Let's make this thing - whatever it is.

Development

This was new territory for us, we imagined that because there is no script to learn for an improvised show, what you must have to learn are the rules. Establishing the rules was our first task.

Early in rehearsals we imagined each performance in a new fictional setting. One night could be Hospital Radio, the next night could be Corporate Radio from a DIY shop, there could be Revolution Radio etc. However, practice revealed that this approach shut down more possibilities than it opened up, themes were much more helpful.

Our initial idea, to have the presenter and producer as characters on stage was soon replaced by the more dynamic arrangement of having two presenters on stage supported by a silent off-stage producer. Following this decision, divisions of labour become clear.

The actors were in charge of everything the audience could hear, both on stage and online. Sitting side by side centre stage at a large office desk they each had their own laptop and microphone. Their laptops were loaded with music including long instrumental tracks and stings for Radio Z. With a mixer inset in the desk between them they chose what music to play and whose voice could be heard at home. In addition, Craig learnt to use a digital 'loop station' that could capture sections of audio and loop them round and round as desired.

Lighting designer Paul Arvidson toured with the show and improvised its lighting states throughout. At this time cheap LED theatre lanterns had just come on the market, by varying the balance within a matrix of red, green and blue bulbs, each lantern could emit in any coloured light across the rainbow. Paul persuaded us to buy and tour with our own set, to give us maximum control.

We called in musician, sound engineer, studio manager and sometime coder Jon Ward to build our onstage radio studio, record Radio Z stings and code the message board that would allow audiences to contribute to the show. Jon helped us to work out a system through which the producer could see messages coming in from the audience, choose what to make public and what sub-set of these messages to send to the performers' screens on stage. By splitting these categories the performers wouldn't be overwhelmed with material or distracted by unhelpful contributions. An option was also created allowing the producer to send messages to the cast on stage that couldn't be seen by the public..

Originally it was planned to have this message board projected on an upstage screen throughout the show, but this seemed both dull and a missed opportunity. By buying a cheap vision mixer and hooking it up to a second laptop we developed the capacity to bring the message board in and out and replace it with video footage or photograph. This visual material gathered in advance or pulled live from the internet within the show could be manipulated using basic VJ software. Managing the message board and the screen was part of the producer's role.

Eventually all this technology started to make the show feel too digital and functional. We needed something poetic to put a spin on the show and make the live experience special in a secret way the remote audience would never know about. To this end at each venue we recruited volunteers to sleep on stage through the show.

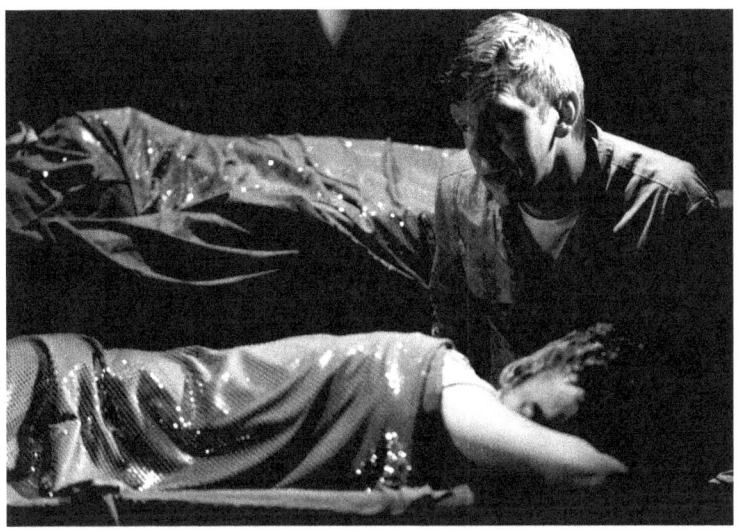

Sleeper Instructions For Tuning Out With Radio Z

The Studio – Warwick Arts Centre
19:45 – 21:45 Tuesday 29th July

Dear XXXXX,

Thank you very much for volunteering to be part of our show.

Tuning Out With Radio Z is about a late night radio programme and how the presenters seek to help people through the night. You, The Sleepers, though appearing not to do anything but sleep, represent many people through the show. Sometimes you will be anonymous figures in the city, sometimes the performers, Amanda and Craig, may choose to imagine you as a particular group of people or specific imaginary individuals. They may pretend to be reading your dreams or living your pasts or futures. They may put extra sheets on you.

In theory you should be asleep throughout the production. In practice you may find the music too loud or that Amanda and Craig start shouting. The show is designed to work as a radio programme so it should be entertaining even if you can't see it, so if you can't sleep please just pretend to be asleep! Being a bit restless at times is fine.

The show is improvised afresh each night so there is a certain unpredictability built in. The performers may appear to be asking you to do something "get up get up!". Ignore anything they say to you unless they make clear it is a stage direction by adding the phrase "for real" within the instruction. It would be good if you could go to the toilet so you don't have to go during the show, if this doesn't work out and you still need to go then the performers will have to adapt and weave your departure into the show. Unless told otherwise, once you leave the stage in this circumstance you shouldn't return.

Please bring some modest nightclothes to wear on stage. It would be great if you could come and find us in the Studio at Warwick Arts Centre at 19:00, this is a bit early but will calm our nerves that you are around.

With thanks again. We look forward to meeting you.

James Yarker for Stan's Cafe

Logic
The logic we built for our performance is that *Tuning Out* fills the overnight slot at Radio Z and its job is to help its listeners safely through the night, no matter what the perils may be.

We agreed that the show's conclusion should always be time based and that the final moment would often be the next DJ coming on to start the programme after *Tuning Out* (this role would be performed by the producer). Paul would fade the video projector to black along with his final lighting state.

Duration
To start with the show was six hours long, this included a two hour stretch at the start which was exclusively webcast, just music played out by Jon. This choice fulfilled our ambition for audiences to be able to start listening to the show at home and continue to listening to it while traveling to the venue before joining it live in the auditorium. At mac the online stream was audible in the foyer, cafe and bar.

Initially the show's live action element lasted four hours. We wanted it to be long enough that people would let go of the structural expectations they have for a show's rhythm and be forced to watch it through a different aesthetic lens. We wanted audiences to live in the show, become habituated to it and exhausted by it, so that on leaving the theatre they would feel they had lived through something and that the outside world would feel like a different - no longer real - world.

Theatrical improvisation is mostly packaged as 'Improv', with an emphasis on technique and wit, quips, gags and quick pay-offs. Spontaneity of creation tends to be mirrored with a ephemerality of effect. On television we encounter this material edited down to a concentrated sub-thirty minute blast. We knew our thing was different and would need longer to evolve. We needed to remove our show far from any familiar 'Improv' format, so it would not be judged by criteria it was not seeking to fulfil.

The show's premise wouldn't allow for an interval but four hours without is a stretch, so we resorted to wristbands allowing audiences to come and go as they pleased.

After the premiere shows at mac we re-evaluated some of our thinking. Most importantly, we had to acknowledge our naïveté in, thinking that local audiences would pass up a free audio version of the show, listened to at home, in favour of a much better full version they had to travel to and pay for. We also recognised both that four hours was unnecessarily long and that, weirdly, even though the show was not plotted in any conventional sense, missing any of it was always to miss something crucial.

In response, for subsequent performances we cut the two hour pre-show broadcast and cut any mention of a 'listen at home' option to local audiences and pushed this exclusively to our remote digital followers. We also cut the show's running time to a more bladder friendly three hours, cut the wristbands and any suggestion audiences may wish to come and go as they pleased..

Tuning out With Radio Z: Technical Specifications

Lighting: see attached lighting plan

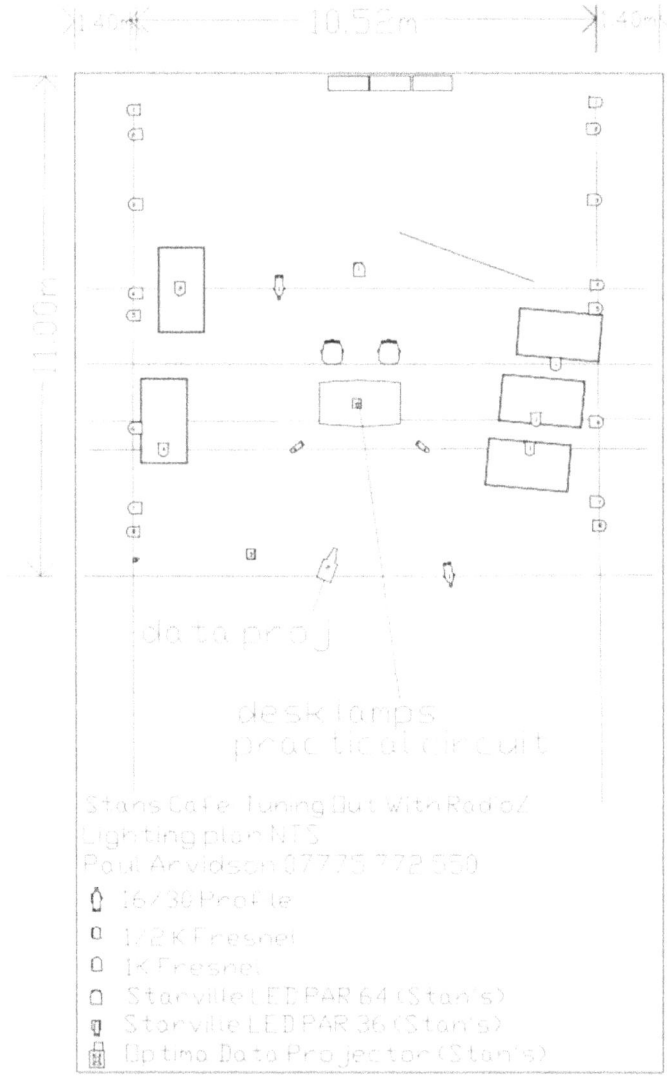

We will require the following:
6 x 1k Fresnels with barndoors to be set at 'head' height (as per LX plan)
5 x 1k Fresnels with barndoors to be rigged overhead, over beds (as per LX plan)
2 x short throw zoom profiles (as per LX plan)
1 x 1/2k Fresnel on 'turtle' or similar low floor-stand
1 x CS onstage lx circuit (preferably ending in 13amp socket) to dim 2 desk-lamps
1 DMX lighting desk with reasonable sized fader wing and second DMX route out of desk (can be same universe).

We will bring:
11 x stairville led par 64s
1 x maplin led par 56
2 x stairville led par 36s
2 x desk lamps (to go into one of your dimmers, see above)
All dmx and mains for same.

Sound:
We will require the following:
1 x reasonable sounding PA system including some form of onstage fold-back for performers.
2 x onstage inputs into your system from our onstage desk (at line level).

We will bring:
1 x self-contained 'radio station' onstage desk including 2 x mics, headphones, pc inputs, macbooks, compressors, pre-amps etc.

AV/other:
We will require the following:
2 x 'always on' computer internet connections: 1 x to be centre-stage for our onstage desk, 1 x to be in your control room near the lighting and sound desks.
1 x control position with enough room to sit 3 x macbooks and some screens near to the lighting and sound positions.

We will bring:
1 x optima data projector to fly from your grid/bars (has safety points etc)
1 x 12' by 9' fastfold screen
5 x big metal beds
3 x metal shelves, 1 x 6' table.

Things you should know:
The show is improvised for its entire length (Lighting, sound and AV included). Under these circumstances it would be nice if usual 'no food and drink in box rules can be relaxed.
The actors have many different props to use during this show, some all or none of which may be used.
Relevant ones to your health and safety brief are:
Prop gun
Water
Stage blood
Kettle (used on-stage halfway through show as the performers make themselves a cup of tea)

Miscellaneous:
The LED's may be used (though not definitely, see improvising note above) to create strobing effects. All the latest guidelines will be followed in their use.

Any queries, please don't hesitate to contact:
Paul Arvidson LD and Stan's Cafe technician.

Performing Tuning Out With Radio Z

When I was a child growing up in the countryside in the late 1970s and early '80s there wasn't much going on and I was also a bit of a loner, so during school holidays I often had to make my own entertainment. In my bedroom I set up Craig's Radio, a small local station which broadcast only to me. I had two tape players, a mono record player and a pair of headphones. My music collection was fairly limited - a lot of Adam and the Ants records and quite a few cassette tapes of chart hits, recorded from Top of the Pops by putting my tape recorder in front of the TV speaker on a Thursday night. With this simple set up I would craft 45 minutes of radio gold (recorded on one side of a C90 tape) creating a show which included music, imaginary shout outs, weather reports, a quiz and an advice slot (the only advice I could genuinely have offered would be how to make your own entertainment on limited resources). I never did make it to broadcasting on Radio 1 or my local radio but to some extent *Tuning Out With Radio Z* saw my childhood ambition realised.

My love of radio has sustained into adulthood - I still listen a lot, often falling asleep to late night programmes with a special speaker that sits under my pillow, so as not to disturb my wife. It's a powerful medium - intimately connecting the broadcaster and the listener in a way that television cannot. In the world of Radio Z we wanted to explore that relationship and the power of the human voice as it drifts over the airwaves offering late night comfort and friendship, soothing anxieties, offering support.

In some ways radio and theatre feel like a good match. They are both live and immediate and they both require their audiences to work a little harder than they might have to while watching film or television. The radio listener must use their imagination, fill in the gaps, visualise what is being described. As a theatre company we talk a lot about our relationship to our audiences. We try to create work in which they must be active, not in a getting up on stage, joining in way, but to be actively engaged intellectually and emotionally. We like to leave space for the audience to bring their own thoughts and experiences to what they are seeing, to join the dots, find their own way through, come to their own conclusions. In *Tuning Out With Radio Z* we wanted this active engagement to become genuine collaboration. And we were interested in how two of our favourite forms might combine - which led us to have two audiences - one in the theatre and one listening remotely online. Since my childhood radio days technology had moved on - a lot. These innovations made *Tuning Out With Radio Z* possible and helped to shape how we thought about and made the show. It was relatively easy to stream audio online, mobile phones allowed people to communicate with us in real time, via texts, whilst sitting in the theatre and an online forum could be read and contributed to by people listening at home. These devices we hoped would connect us with the audiences and give them the opportunity to help co-author the performance.

Every performance of *Tuning Out With Radio Z* was improvised, devised afresh each night. This made devising and rehearsing the show rather difficult. Initially we played around with the radio station being set in a particular context or location - a hospital, a secret organisation, on a cruise ship. These were often fun to explore but seemed to close down possibilities rather than open them up. None of that early experimentation was wasted though - some of what we explored inevitably found its way into the subsequent performances even if we weren't aware of it. In the end the rehearsal process became one of developing a set of rules and parameters within which we could operate. We agreed on techniques and strategies we could employ to create material in the moment. We trawled through our prop store to pull out things that we thought might be useful - everything from party poppers to a stethoscope; from glow sticks to tins of soup and of course a kettle to make tea. Most of these objects were, at some point, pressed into service, although I don't think we ever had a tin opener for the soup.

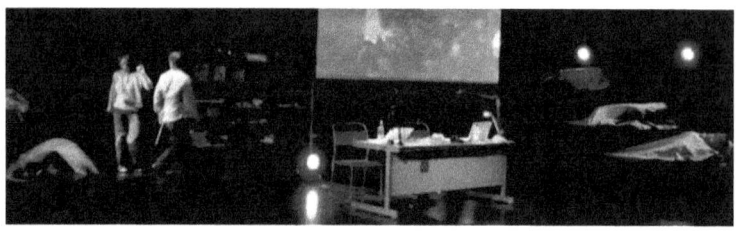

Part of the idea behind *Tuning Out With Radio Z* was to put our devising process on stage, for an audience. Usually the devising process takes place behind closed doors, occasionally with guests invited in to watch. In that context as a performer you have licence to try stuff out, to experiment, to make a fool of yourself in front of your fellow performers. The good stuff might make it through, anything that doesn't quite work or doesn't fit is left on the cutting room floor and forgotten about. The really bad stuff becomes the stuff of company legend but is thankfully never seen by an audience. In *Tuning Out With Radio Z*, however there was nowhere to hide and everything was witnessed. It was one of our most challenging shows to perform in, devising a new show each night, live in front of not one but two audiences.

Each performance started with a theme, given to us by James earlier in the day. The theme was just a word …Lost, Flood, Ghost. We would then have a couple of hours before the show to think, to share ideas and to do some research online to gather some material. By the start of the show we would each have a small collection of thoughts and material to give us starting points. These could be literary, artistic, historic, musical or personal memories. We would rewrite the days news headlines and weather reports into our house style so by the time the show started we would have some fragments ready to be collaged together. We wanted to be prepared but not too prepared, to have somewhere to start but leave room for contributions from the audiences, to give them the opportunity to help shape the content and direction of each performance.

As performers we placed a lot of trust in each other. When the show started we knew we just had each other, alone on the stage with 3 or 4 hours to work together and create something out of almost nothing. It was a scary, exciting ride, building on each others contributions, spotting when your fellow performer was onto something, helping them build it or dropping back to allow them to go for it, being ready to bail them out when they got stuck or lost. We had two worlds to balance - the theatre world and the radio world - we had stage time and air time to fill. We were anxious that there shouldn't be any dead air. We were careful to ensure that we treated audience contributions with respect. Both we and the audience had to discover the rules of engagement - we didn't always want to simply read out their contributions, we wanted to weave them into fictions, have them detonate further into the performance, take us down routes we wouldn't have thought of. This was a big ask for them (and for us). We would try to structure the piece as we went, using the radio time check as a means to refocus, move us forward or get us out of a dead end. We would try to see ahead - ten minutes, thirty minutes, two hours in an attempt to impose some sort of shape, to bring in changes of tone and pace, to have some light and shade. When it worked it was thrilling. Near the end of one show Graeme and I got a small cheer from

closely and spotted that after three hours we had somehow managed to bring a story that had developed between the two of us to a conclusion. I'm not sure we even realised how we had done it. There were also moments when we knew that we were adrift, struggling to keep the whole thing going, battling to keep our audiences with us. In some ways thought this was part of it - part of the world of our fictional radio presenter selves - struggling to keep broadcasting and provide that voice of calm in a world of anxiety and chaos.

At its best the show conjured worlds and fictions from our very limited resources, from our voices and our audiences' contributions. Our listeners and the onstage sleepers became our family, long lost friends, lovers, late night revellers, protagonists in unseen dramas. They were the missing, the lost and lonely, victims of war or disasters, inventors, heroes and friends.

Perhaps the shows were too long. Perhaps they weren't long enough. But each show did feel like a shared achievement. We and the audience had been through something together, had connected for a few hours. across the airwaves and the proscenium arch.

Craig Stephens, March 2020

cafe

A mac commission

RADIO Z IS THE LAST STATION ON THE DIAL. 'Tuning Out' is its late night show and no two nights are ever the same. Each show brings fresh challenges for the two presenters, new opportunities and unexpected crises. News breaks, personal issues well up and messages stream in from 'out there' and they must juggle it all. They never know what will happen next, but they know they must keep us safe, solve the riddles of the night and chart a course for dawn. They must be professional, no matter what...

Tuning Out With Radio Z is a bold new theatre adventure waiting to be created by you and Stan's Cafe. Improvised afresh each night, this epic show is designed to be co-written live, with its audience submitting material by text message, e-mail or the message board at www.radioz.co.uk. A genuine radio show, 'Tuning Out' can be heard on-line at home or on the move but the real action takes place in the theatre.

As it's improvised, any promises as to what the show will contain would be unwise, but it should make you think and humand laugh. Who knows, it may even make you gasp or cry or dance. It may provoke you to write some material and glory in hearing it woven into the unspooling narrative. You will be issued with a wristband, so you can create your own intervals, if you're too tired to stay to the finale at home in bed, but we believe that once you are in the studio with the presenters you won't want to leave.

In order to submit material to the show you are welcome to bring phones or laptops into the theatre. Staff in mac's New Media suite will also be happy to help you contribute on-line.

13th May 17:00 – 23:00
14th May 19:00 – 01:00
15th May 17:00 – 23:00

13th May 19:00 – 23:00
14th May 21:00 – 01:00
15th May 19:00 – 23:00

mac, Cannon Hill Park, Birmingham B12 9QH
Tickets £12(£9)
Sales 01214463232 or www.macarts.co.uk

Birmingham City Council

  ARTS COUNCIL ENGLAND

stan's cape

TUNING OUT WITH RADIO Z

a **mac** commission

Devising	Amanda Hadingue & Craig Stephens
Improvised in Dartington by	Bernadette Russell & Craig Stephens
VJ improvisation	Liam D'Authreau
At home	James Yarker
Studio construction, station branding & software	Jon Ward
Lighting design & improvisation	Paul Arvidson
Photographs & Video	Various Artists
Graphic design	Simon Ford
Production Assistants	Esther Belvis Pons
	Diego Alejandro de la Vega Wood
General Manager	Charlotte Martin
Advisory Producer	Nick Sweeting

With thanks to:
Tonight's Sleepers
Rhubarb Radio (especially Peter Dickson) and A E Harris & Co. (Birmingham) Ltd. for their help
Mick the Roadie. Everyone at the office and mac for keeping the faith.

Programme Notes.
I don't normally hold with extensive programme notes as I believe shows should be able to speak for themselves. However, in order for you to get the most from this show, there are some things it would be good for you to know in advance, so here are some notes.

Your Contribution.
Everything happening tonight is improvised. Nothing is rehearsed in advance. A theme is agreed, usually the day before – tonight's theme is EARTH - but all other choices, including what music to play, are made by the actors during the show. There is plenty of room for your contributions to influence those choices.

- **Please leave your mobile phones ON**, turn them to silent and text contributions to the show on: 07580 631888 (please don't attach photos)

- **Contribute On-line** via the newsroom at www.radioz.co.uk, where you can see what is coming into the show and how it is being processed.

- **e-mail** the show directly using news@radioz.co.uk.

If there is Wi-Fi at the venue there will be notices around to help you gain access to it.

"There is probably no more interesting company working in the UK today"
Lynn Gardner in The Guardian

What To Contribute?

Our ambition is that you write the show with us. The actors working in character will invite a certain range of contributions, but there are many other levels of contribution possible. You may send news updates, traffic or weather reports to the show. You may source photos or send links to video streams for the screen. You may write more provocative or poetic text. You may have suggestions that shift the show's tone, direction or narrative. You can contribute as different people with different populations. You can build on or respond to the work of other people. Your material will be collated and fed to the actors.

Why Improvisation?

Improvisation is a technique we use regularly in private to test out ideas and generate material for new shows. Over the years I have been privileged to sit as solitary witness to many, many hours of improvisation. These improvisations are not theatre games but experiments and, as with all experiments, sometimes they succeed and sometimes they don't. Usually you learn something, and occasionally you witness a transcendental moment when something sparks and a breathtaking, illuminating theatrical phenomenon occurs. Unfortunately, it is always more difficult to capture these moments and repeat them in a show than it is to create them in the first place. Often I have wished there was an audience in the rehearsal room to share this excitement with. Now we have made the improvisation the show. Tonight you are sure to see small-scale experiments succeeding and failing. We hope that you consider this show-scale experiment a success, or at the very least an enjoyable failure.

Remember it's all improvised and you can improvise too.

"At the heart of most of Stan's Cafe's works there is a simple idea, which is then pursued with an extreme boldness bordering on recklessness."

David Tushingham: Festwoch Wein

Why So Long?

We don't want this show to be watched in a conventional way, so we have extended its duration to do away with conventional rhythms. There is no interval, so if you need a break just choose your moment and if you need to go home before it's finished you can listen on to the conclusion via www.radioz.co.uk. In practice, we hope you stay forever – or at least until the end.

Other Things.

Please feel free to take photographs (no flashes please). You are welcome to share them on the web, but please do not post them whilst the show is running as we want you, the live audience, with exclusive access to the show's visual material.

Please don't shoot video of the show (theatre always looks so RUBBISH on video).

Thanks for coming.

James Yarker   www.stanscafe.co.uk

Warwick Arts Centre Playlists

Saturday 16th October

ARTIST	TRACK
Blur	To The End
Another Fine Day	So Blue
John Cale & Terry Riley	Ides Of March
LCD Soundsystem	Innocuous! (Soulwax Remix)
Wim Mertens	Whisper Me
David Bowie	Wild Is The Wind
Elvis Costello	I Can't Stand Up For Falling Down
The Chemical Brothers	The Big Jump
Tortoise	Djed
The Beatles	If I Fell
Jon Hopkins	Light Through The Veins
The Fall	Lost In Music
Electric Light Orchestra	Sweet Is The Night
Japan	Quiet Life
Spiro	The Radio Sky

Friday 15th October

ARTIST	TRACK
Massive Attack	Unfinished Sympathy
Nancy Sinatra & Lee Hazlewood	Some Velvet Morning
Jimi Hendrix	Little Wing
Modified Toy Orchestra	Electric Rapture Because Of You
The Necks	Unheard
Nusrat Fateh Ali Kahn & Michael Brook	Night Song
Six Organs Of Admittance	School Of The Flower
Wim Mertens	Mystik
Yo La Tengo	Moonrock Mambo
Steve Reich	Six Pianos
Kraftwerk	Airwaves
Super Furry Animals	Frequency
T. Rex	New York City
Prince Buster	Too Hot

Thursday 14th October

ARTIST	TRACK
Lester Bowie's Brass Fantasy	I Only Have Eyes For You
Public Enemy	Party For Your Right To Fight
Primal Scream	Loaded
The White Stripes	Seven Nation Army
Patti Smith	Babelogue
The Smiths	William, It Was Really Nothing
Popul Vuh	Take The Tention High
The Velvet Underground	I'm Sticking With You
Icebreaker International	Port Of Rotterdam
The Cardigans	Tomorrow
Yo La Tengo	Pass The Hatchet, I Think I'm Goodkind
Prince	Sign "O" The Times
Ibrahim Ferrer	Herido De Sombras
Buena Vista Social Club	Dos Gardenias

Reviews

"In a the middle of a hamstrung nation the calming voices of Craig and Amanda sooth us through three hours of bleak twilight before dawn breaks on a brave new world. *Tuning Out With Radio Z* is a prolonged and diaphanous experience which eerily looks at loss; a diluted journey where occasionally items of improvised and crafted brilliance spring out of the dullness of waiting. Intrigued in this monotony Stan's Cafe include no interval in their marathon instead providing wristbands enabling you to take breaks, wittily stemming modern panic."

Honour Bayes

"Something rarely tolerated in improvised theatre is slow improvised theatre. It needs to be snappy because no one wants to wait around in the hope that something might happen."

Naima Khan

"It's appropriate that Radio Z asks more questions than it answers. I've expended hundreds of words on it and I haven't really gotten on to those sleeping people, or the moment I realised that there was a retelling of Orpheus and Eurydice going on, or on my take about what the show was about (I'm not saying exactly what this is because I think everyone should be able to make their own version, using their imagination as well as their phones - but I will say that the clue is in the title). I haven't written about how interesting I found watching what the director chose to publish on the forum or the fact that though you were allowed to come in and out of the performance I sat through all three hours without once feeling the need to move. I haven't even written about fear or joy or pain, all of which Radio Z evoked for me."

Corinne Furness

Blog Post

This show's a monster, impossible to tame and if tamed, pointless. Tonight's theme is LUCK and it's against us. FOH foul up: programmes – key instructions for audience collaboration – haven't been distributed. SMS to Web translation apparatchik hits glitch, backstage phone support required. Now audience messages start to flow, cue laughs of recognition. Amanda and Craig – Radio Presenters – are on good banter form. The show even turns French for a period, they can keep this fun up for ever but it needs to escape and transcend and tonight we're struggling with that.

I'm placing still images and video behind the improvisation, likely material ripped from YouTube. 'Lucky people' footage causes gasps but is perhaps too obvious, the 'lighthouse beam' feels better but nothing's really meshing. I want to catalyse a transformation and so, via web and stage screen, solicit audience help. With honourable exceptions incoming is standard radio shtick – maybe tonight's theme is badly chosen. In the rehearsal room you would stop, adjust, reset and re-launch, but here the train can't stop until the end of the line. I'm growing desperate, pulling and pushing leavers, all feels futile. It's Stan's Cafe's job to experiment but right now this it feels like it's blowing up in our faces.

Stage sleepers fail to find a place in the broader fiction, two didn't show and now, maybe two hours in, an audience message arrives requesting to join their number. Why not? I get them backstage and brief them. Shocked but game, their arrival provides strong raw material and we get into some good stuff. The closing passages are moving – a quality familiar with epic long shows. It's over.

Maybe this observation changed the observed; 'tomorrow night is bound to be a triumph'. It is. A validation of the enterprise, shared only with those who are present, such is the joy of the improvised.

16th October, 2010

Notes On Video For Liam

Liam d'Authreau was the VJ who had solved all the technical challenges we faced trying to share and mix a variety of video sources with our audience. When there came a gig I couldn't attend, so we asked Liam to take on the video mixing. At home, listening online, I would continue to play role of producer with the message board. Our friend Peter had the Stan's Cafe burner phone to convert SMS messages into emails for us. Below are notes briefing Liam on how the video the worked in the show by late in the tour.

"Screen action is supposed to compliment stage action in *Radio Z*. The only instances in which it should fully draw focus are when displaying the News Room. It should render itself a layer of 'text' by being slow, still or repetitive.

In the show characters cannot see the screen and in reality the performers are only occasionally vaguely aware of what is being projected. The screen can act as a landscape for the physical action or look to set up a poetic resonance with it.

The show is improvised but a number of rules / strategies have emerged for the use of the screen.

1: I always open with photo of the Radio Z logo screwed to the door of our rehearsal space.

2: Once the audience are in and settled and whilst some music is playing early on I show The News Room and a message from The Producer welcoming everyone to the show and sharing with them what the night's theme is.

3: There is a 'bin' of images called Studio these form the vocabulary of images used when the performers are back in relatively 'normal' Radio Studio mode. My principle image is of a microphone but I use a variety either to keep things fresh or to pull focus to a particular aspect of the studio, The Phone, A List of Possible Topics Etc. There is a long shot of the performance table in a rehearsal room, I particularly like using this to undermine the stability of the radio station or to reinforce moments when there is a glitch in the identity of the station of its inhabitants.

4: Early in the show, when requests have come in, I like to bring up a feature in the News Room that 'proves' that requests are coming through and being acted upon. My basic rule is that going to and from the News Room is a push transition on the vision mixer but all other transitions are dissolves.

5: Your theme on Thursday is EARTH. I generally do an hour or two of prep in which I seek to gather material which may be useful for this theme. It is usually video footage ripped from the web but I have been known to run around taking still photographs of things.

For EARTH I would imagine obviously some of the following being useful: views of The Earth from space; images of soil; a graveyard / grave stones; flowers, possibly swaying in the wind; maybe some images of ploughing or mechanical diggers; maybe images of birds flocking around freshly ploughed soil; worms wriggling; a time lapse shot of a field; one of those races people do through mud.

I often don't have a great deal to run with when the show starts and often I spend effort getting images and not using any of them because the improvisation sets off in a direction that doesn't lend itself to the images. Usefully there is a growing library of images used in previous shows that can be reused.

Early shows used to rely predominantly on still images, later video loops came to dominate, now I feel I'm either striking a balance or taking each new show on merit of what it needs.

6: Sometimes the screen responds to what is going on with the performers, occasionally I try and anticipate what they may be about to do and put up an image that isn't directly linked to what is currently going on – often it gains its own logic over time, sometimes you have to admit defeat and withdraw an image, I try not to do this without giving the image a good chance to work / accrete meaning.

7: Accreting meaning is a useful thing. If an image seems to chime strongly with some powerful material being performed I will look to turn this image into a motif within the show by returning to it periodically. This image comes to symbolise something for me, often something that is difficult to articulate. This strategy is an attempt to give the extended improvisation an added coherence / sense of structure.

8: Mostly I try not to use fictional or known material in the show. For the theme FOOL I used a small clip from an old slapstick film but mostly I don't like the thought of this screen bringing in references to other art works.

9: I tend to put the laptop running the Resolume VJ software on the right and on left a second laptop running other programs, between them, if there is space goes the vision mixer. As video mixing still isn't a big part of the theatrical vocabulary I am often squeezed for space and the vision mixer has to go behind the laptops. The left hand machine is on-line. I use this to run the News Room. It is good, intermittently, to remind the audience of the News Room as a motor behind the show.

Occasionally I make direct appeals to the live audience for material signing myself as The Producer. I may post some of these 'For The Audience' messages remotely for you to put up at a time when you feel they won't be too intrusive. I like typing these messages with the News Room on screen so there is a live 'teleprinter' feel to them, but this will be impossible on Thursday.

10: I also use the left hand laptop for screening stuff directly from the web. This may be clips from YouTube in full screen mode (it's an art mixing away from them before they end and reveal their source). Google Earth can often be helpful, I will occasionally zoom right in and do searches, or pull further out and drift over landscapes or oceans. There may be more specific 'real time' elements that are helpful, for example I have occasionally used sites that track aircraft or shipping movements. My ambition of logging onto dull webcams of street scenes around the world is usually thwarted.

11: I have started to find the Freeze function on the scan converters increasingly useful, particularly for the left hand computer as it gives me cover for more research, looping or other ugly activities that need to be hidden. It sometimes also helps with the right hand computer when I get the sense Resolume is about to crash.

12: At the end of the show I return to the 'Radio Z sign on door' image, usually the slightly wider version that shows the wall which the door is set in. I will then fade the screen to black using the vision mixer as the desk lights are faded. If I have gone on stage to end the show as the next DJ starting his program Paul will do this final fade for me.

Themes and Actors

Lost: Amanda Hadingue & Craig Stephens

Flood: Amanda Hadingue & Craig Stephens

Shooting: Amanda Hadingue & Craig Stephens

Escape: Amanda Hadingue & Craig Stephens

Cure: Amanda Hadingue & Craig Stephens

Revolution: Amanda Hadingue & Craig Stephens

Electricity: Amanda Hadingue & Craig Stephens

Luck: Amanda Hadingue & Craig Stephens

Fever: Amanda Hadingue & Craig Stephens

Fall: Amanda Hadingue & Craig Stephens

Sea: Amanda Hadingue & Craig Stephens

Ghost: Bernadette Russell & Craig Stephens

Freeze: Bernadette Russell & Craig Stephens

Flight: Graeme Rose & Craig Stephens

Money: Graeme Rose & Craig Stephens

Paranoia: Graeme Rose & Craig Stephens

Fool: Bernadette Russell & Craig Stephens

Earth: Bernadette Russell & Craig Stephens

Borders: Amanda Hadingue & Craig Stephens

About the illustration and design

The illustrations for the covers of these books were undertaken by students at Birmingham City University as the final module of their first-year illustration course during the Spring/Summer of 2018. The images were developed using workshops using variations of the theatre-devising methods produced by Stan's Cafe but adapted and applied to the making of visual work. The resulting work was shown in the pop-up exhibition *The Something Of Somebody Something* at AE Harris in May 2018.

The design concept of the books was produced by final year Graphic Design student Aimee Chapman. These were then further developed for print in a collaborative process between Stan's Cafe and the University's Innovation Product Support Service (IPSS) and involved helping the company with selecting appropriate DTP software, undertaking training and selecting a suitable print on demand service.

Gareth Courage
Lecturer in Illustration
Birmingham City University

www.ingramcontent.com/pod-product-compliance
Lightning Source LLC
Chambersburg PA
CBHW071751080526
44588CB00013B/2216